This book belongs to

Copyright © 2020

Disclaimer
All Rights Reserved. No part of this book may be reproduced or transmitted in any form or by any means, mechanical or electronic, including photocopying or recording, or by any information storage and retrieval system, or transmitted by email without permission in writing from the publisher. This book is for entertainment purposes only. The views expressed are those of the author alone.

SAMPLE IMAGES

ALLOSAURUS	**APATOSAURUS**	**ARCHAEOPTERYX**
BRACHIOSAURUS	**DILOPHOSAURUS**	**SPINOSAURUS**
STEGOSAURUS	**TRICERATOPS**	**TYRANNOSAURUS REX**

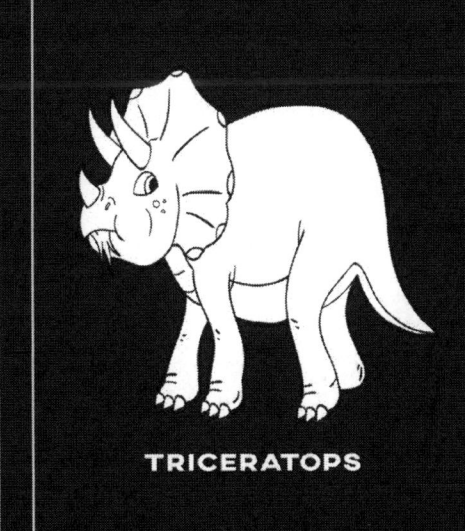

SAMPLE IMAGES

VELOCIRAPTOR	ALLOSAURUS	APATOSAURUS
ARCHAEOPTERYX	BRACHIOSAURUS	DILOPHOSAURUS
SPINOSAURUS	STEGOSAURUS	TRICERATOPS

SAMPLE IMAGES

TYRANNOSAURUS REX	VELOCIRAPTOR	ALLOSAURUS
APATOSAURUS	ARCHAEOPTERYX	BRACHIOSAURUS
DILOPHOSAURUS	SPINOSAURUS	STEGOSAURUS

ALLOSAURUS

BLANK PAGE
(Page kept blank in case of bleeding through coloring from the previous page.
Use this page for drawing

APATOSAURUS

BLANK PAGE

(Page kept blank in case of bleeding through coloring from the previous page.

Use this page for drawing

ARCHAEOPTERYX

BLANK PAGE
(Page kept blank in case of bleeding through coloring from the previous page.
Use this page for drawing

BRACHIOSAURUS

BLANK PAGE

(Page kept blank in case of bleeding through coloring from the previous page.

Use this page for drawing

DILOPHOSAURUS

BLANK PAGE
(Page kept blank in case of bleeding through coloring from the previous page.
Use this page for drawing

BLANK PAGE
(Page kept blank in case of bleeding through coloring from the previous page.
Use this page for drawing

SPINOSAURUS

BLANK PAGE
(Page kept blank in case of bleeding through coloring from the previous page.
Use this page for drawing

STEGOSAURUS

BLANK PAGE
(Page kept blank in case of bleeding through coloring from the previous page.
Use this page for drawing

TRICERATOPS

BLANK PAGE
(Page kept blank in case of bleeding through coloring from the previous page.
Use this page for drawing

TYRANNOSAURUS REX

BLANK PAGE
(Page kept blank in case of bleeding through coloring from the previous page.
Use this page for drawing

VELOCIRAPTOR

BLANK PAGE
(Page kept blank in case of bleeding through coloring from the previous page.
Use this page for drawing

ALLOSAURUS

BLANK PAGE
(Page kept blank in case of bleeding through coloring from the previous page.
Use this page for drawing

APATOSAURUS

BLANK PAGE
(Page kept blank in case of bleeding through coloring from the previous page.
Use this page for drawing

ARCHAEOPTERYX

BLANK PAGE

(Page kept blank in case of bleeding through coloring from the previous page.

Use this page for drawing

BRACHIOSAURUS

BLANK PAGE

(Page kept blank in case of bleeding through coloring from the previous page.

Use this page for drawing

DILOPHOSAURUS

BLANK PAGE
(Page kept blank in case of bleeding through coloring from the previous page.
Use this page for drawing

SPINOSAURUS

BLANK PAGE
(Page kept blank in case of bleeding through coloring from the previous page.
Use this page for drawing

STEGOSAURUS

BLANK PAGE

(Page kept blank in case of bleeding through coloring from the previous page.

Use this page for drawing

TRICERATOPS

BLANK PAGE
(Page kept blank in case of bleeding through coloring from the previous page.
Use this page for drawing

TYRANNOSAURUS REX

BLANK PAGE
(Page kept blank in case of bleeding through coloring from the previous page.
Use this page for drawing

VELOCIRAPTOR

BLANK PAGE

(Page kept blank in case of bleeding through coloring from the previous page.

Use this page for drawing

ALLOSAURUS

BLANK PAGE
(Page kept blank in case of bleeding through coloring from the previous page.
Use this page for drawing

APATOSAURUS

BLANK PAGE
(Page kept blank in case of bleeding through coloring from the previous page.
Use this page for drawing

ARCHAEOPTERYX

BLANK PAGE

(Page kept blank in case of bleeding through coloring from the previous page.

Use this page for drawing

BRACHIOSAURUS

BLANK PAGE
(Page kept blank in case of bleeding through coloring from the previous page.
Use this page for drawing

DILOPHOSAURUS

BLANK PAGE
(Page kept blank in case of bleeding through coloring from the previous page.
Use this page for drawing

SPINOSAURUS

BLANK PAGE
(Page kept blank in case of bleeding through coloring from the previous page.
Use this page for drawing

STEGOSAURUS

BLANK PAGE
(Page kept blank in case of bleeding through coloring from the previous page.
Use this page for drawing

TRICERTOPS

BLANK PAGE
(Page kept blank in case of bleeding through coloring from the previous page.
Use this page for drawing

TYRANNOSAURUS REX

SKETCHING PAGE

SKETCHING PAGE

SKETCHING PAGE

SKETCHING PAGE

SKETCHING PAGE

SKETCHING PAGE

SKETCHING PAGE

SKETCHING PAGE

SKETCHING PAGE

SKETCHING PAGE

SKETCHING PAGE

SKETCHING PAGE

SKETCHING PAGE

SKETCHING PAGE

SKETCHING PAGE

SKETCHING PAGE

SKETCHING PAGE

SKETCHING PAGE

Manufactured by Amazon.ca
Bolton, ON